KEEPING PEAFOWL

BY

JAMES BLAKE

NIMROD PRESS LTD
15 THE MALTINGS
TURK ST
ALTON GU34 1DL
HAMPSHIRE

ISBN 1-85259- 069- 6

NIMROD PRESS LTD
15 The Maltings
Turk Street
Alton,Hants, GU34 1DL

KEEPING

PEAFOWL

i

OTHER TITLES AVAILABLE OR IN PRODUCTION

CONTENTS

LIST OF ILLUSTRATIONS

COLOURED PLATES

One of the plates overleaf has an interesting history. Charles M. Inglis, Curator, Darjeeling Natural History Museum was not satisfied with the illustration of the two species shown in the book: " The Game Birds of India, Burmah and Ceylon" by Hume and Marshall and he therefore substituted his own painting.

Green Peafowl
Pavo muticus

Blue Peafowl (Indian)
Pavo cristatus

Comparison of Main Species of Peafowl (1/6 size). Painted by C.M. Inglis, MBOU, FZS, IFES, Late Curator, Darjeeling Natural History Museum.

Spalding Hen (*Pavo* *muticus* × *cristatus*) with chicks of three months old.

1
INTRODUCING PEAFOWL

Figure 1-1 Tail of Peafowl with Train extended

Figure 1-2 Display of the White Peacock

KEEPING PEAFOWL

INTRODUCING PEAFOWL

THE FAMILY STRUCTURE

Peafowl belong to the Order of birds known as GALLI-FORMES and are part of the Pheasant family (Phasianidae) which also includes;

(a) domestic poultry
(b) jungle fowl
(c) quail and other game birds

The order GALLIFORMES is made up of the following families:

1. PHASIANIDAE (above)
2. MELEAGRIDEA (Turkeys)
3. NUMIDIDAE (Guinea Fowl)

Peafowl are given a latin name PAVO which is then followed by the species; e.g. PAVO CRISTATUS* is the Common Blue Peafowl. A distinctive feature of the peafowl is the crest, discussed later.

There are three distinct species and a hybrid (cross):

1. **COMMON BLUE PEAFOWL,** PAVO CRIS-TATUS which originated from India and Sri Lanka. Variations of the common peafowl are:

*The scientific names should be shown as *Pavo cristatus,* but for emphasis have been given capitals.

3

(a) White (hybrid)
(b) Black Winged (or Black Shouldered) (A mutation, PAVO CRISTATUS, NIGRIPENNIS)
(c) Pied (mutation)
(d) Silver Dun (or Cameo)

2. GREEN PEAFOWL; also known as Scaled Peafowl (PAVO MUTICUS) embracing:

(a) Green Java Peafowl (PAVO MUTICUS MUTICUS)
(b) Indo-China Peafowl (PAVO MUTICUS IMPERITON)
(c) Burmese Peafowl (PAVO MUTICUS SPICIFER)

3. SPALDING OR EMERALD PEAFOWL – a hybrid from crossing the two main species MUTICUS and CRISTATUS.

4. CONGO PEAFOWL (AFROPAVO CONGENSIS)

Not all ornithologists agree that the Congo Peafowl is a true Peafowl. Some regard it as a pheasant whereas others suggest it is a variety of Francolin.

They have the distinctive crest of the Peafowl family, but then so do some other Peacock Pheasants. The lack of the large tail or train certainly makes them unusual when compared with conventional peafowl. Moreover they are extremely difficult to rear and until more knowledge is gained are likely to remain in specialist establishments such as bird gardens or zoos.

4

VARIATIONS IN COLOUR (MUTATIONS)

Inevitably, as with any birds kept in captivity, there are "sports" produced. In time ,many variations will be found.

The variations have occurred already in the Indian Peafowl *(Pavocristatus)* and include White, Pied and Black–Winged species.

These varieties are described in more detail in Chapter 6. In the case of the Silver Dun or Cameo we have no direct knowledge of this variety. It is a soft delicate beige in colour and was bred in captivity by Oscar Mulloy (USA) and other collaborators. The development is described in *Peafowl Breeding and Management* by L o y l Stromberg, Stromberg Publishing, Pine River, Minnesota.

THE NAME AND DISTINCTIVE FEATURES

The origin of the name Peafowl is not known with absolute certainty. However, according to Baron Cuvier *(The Animal Kingdom)* the name is derived from their cry ("Paen").

Peafowl have distinctive features which include:

1. Crest or Aigrette which adorns the head and in the Common (Blue) Peafowl widens at the tip; i.e. the vane is at the tip; whereas in the Java (Green) Peafowl the vane runs through the full shaft of the feathers.

2. Tail which may form into a "train" or which may erect into a large "disc" or fan which is broad and upright.

3. Plumage in a mature male which is beautiful and irridescent with silky barbs and eye–like spots of blue, fringed with green.

More details are given in later sections.

PROBLEMS WITH PEAFOWL

Peafowl have been objects of admiration for many centuries. Visitors to modern zoos gaze in wonder as the Peacock shows off with his raised tail and strutting walk. It was because of their exceptional beauty that they were introduced into the west and have been bred there ever since.

Beyond their beauty and the interest of managing them and breeding from them they have little to offer in utility terms. Indeed, it has been stated that it has "the plumage of an angel, the voice of a devil and the guts of a thief". In plain language the Peacock suffers from the following:

1. Shrill piercing shriek which makes it unsuitable for keeping near domestic houses where neighbours object to birds and bird noises.

2. Greed -- eating all to be found whether garden plants, flowers, edible shrubs, etc. This makes Peafowl unsuitable for free range in a garden. They quickly devour all in sight.

In addition, Peafowl bully other birds and if given the opportunity will kill poultry chicks and, in the case of the Peacock, it will eliminate its own offspring. This is why the Peahen finds a secluded spot for her eggs where she cannot be found by the ever-amorous Peacock.

PEAFOWL IN CAPTIVITY

Peafowl came from many parts of the World -- India,

Malaysia, Burma, Siam, Indo China and Africa – where the climate is quite hot. They have acclimatised very well, over thousands of years, with the result that they can now be bred and managed in captivity. However, they are not suitable birds for close confinement. If it is considered that they are many times larger than, say, a pheasant and any accommodation to be suitable should reflect this fact. A typical size is around 2 metres for the male and 1 metre for the female so any aviary must reflect this fact. The Congo Peafowl are smaller (around 67cm for the male who has a relatively short tail). As will be shown later, an aviary is possible, but peafowl thrive best where they can roost in a large shed or barn and have access to a lawn or paddock, adequately fenced, or they will roam.

At this early stage it is necessary to stress that the term "Peafowl" covers:

1. **Peacocks** – easily distinguishable by the magnificent colours and large tail which becomes a "fan" when a male peacock displays (a courtship ritual or simply "showing off").

2. **Peahens** – rather dowdy compared with the cocks but, nevertheless, quite attractive.

The plumage varies according to age. Generally speaking for the first two years the plumage is the same, but in the third year the long dorsal plumes of the male begin to appear. In fact it is in the third year that the hen begins to lay. She may lay upwards of five eggs with a maximum of around twelve. If taken away daily and kept in sawdust she will continue to lay until the batch is "completed". A second batch may be laid later in the season – possibly 3–4 weeks later, but much depends upon whether she is allowed to incubate (see Chapter 5 .

KEEPING PEAFOWL

Mention should be made that the Congo Peafowl does not breed readily in captivity and in many respects is very similar to some of the larger pheasants, being both difficult to manage and breed from. Indeed, discussions on Peafowl do not usually include the Congo Peafowl for the simple reason that they are so relatively new, being discovered in 1936 by Dr. James P. Chapin. Undoubtedly, they should lend themselves to aviary life more readily when breeders have studied their habits more closely.

ESSENTIAL REQUIREMENTS
Like all birds kept in captivity the precise requirements will depend upon the natural food available and if given free access to a grass run will pick up berries, insects, chickweed, grass and various plants so essential to their well-being. If kept in aviaries the food should be adequate to maintain body, feathers and eggs in the breeding season. The requirements for the feeding of Peafowl are covered in Chapter 2.

PROUD AS A PEACOCK
Nature has bestowed upon the Peacock an outstanding beauty in the form of a beautiful head and neck, graceful shape of body and legs and the amazing train of feathers which are used to display the magnificent colours. In addition, it would appear that he has great energy – he requires not less than five wives – and a character which allows him to exhibit to all that he really is the king of birds.

Some writers have agreed that he is no prouder than many other birds. In fact, the Peacock is simply going through a

Figure 1.3 Peacock Pheasant Display

stereotype form of courting display to be found amongst many birds. In technical language the Peacock, like these other birds, is responding to the influence of what are referred to as "gonadotrophic hormones"; i.e., the reproduction process.

Examples of extraordinary courtship displays are:

1. The Tragopan Pheasant
This bird goes through a complex dance with horns and wattles swelling and with wings and tail rising and falling.

2. Peacock Pheasant
Behaves in a manner very similar to the display of the true Peacock. (Figure 1.3)

3. Australian Bustard
Included in its courtship display is a large dilatable pouch (Figure 1.4)

4. Pouter Pigeon
There are many varieties and when they strut they blow out the neck pouch (Figure 1.5)

The Peacock is no more proud than any of these birds, but somehow he has been given the description which makes him appear the supreme example of pride and arrogance.

PEAFOWL AS FOOD
There are many stories of Peafowl being used at banquets both in edible form and as a decoration (preserved and then shown with the plumage exhibited in a special way). It is said the Romans regarded the cooked Peafowl as a great delicacy.

Figure 1.4 Australian Bustard Display

Obviously the culinary art has been lost for later attempts at serving Peafowl as a dish were not very successful. For no apparent reason the Peafowl, unlike the Turkey, has lost favour as a source of food.

Peafowl live to a great age, possibly up to 25 years, so obviously a bird of that age is not likely to be very tender. Normally poultry are eaten at not more than 6 months old. This may be the reason for the poor reputation. In any event if a Peahen produces, say, 10 chicks in a year this is likely to be expensive food and, therefore, not commercially viable.

WHY KEEP PEAFOWL?

If we look for good, sound commercial reasons for keeping Peafowl there are very few.

As indicated, they are not accepted as worthwhile food nor do they produce sufficient eggs to make a venture worthwhile for egg production or for meat.

The main reason for their continued existence as a domesticated bird is the fascination of their great beauty. They adorn parks, zoos, paddocks, farm lands, aviaries with a grace that cannot be matched by even the most splendid pheasant. Moreover, they are domesticated to the extent of being able to let them roam free and they will return to the house or aviary. This would not occur with ornamental pheasants which remain very much semi-wild creatures.

Whilst ever men and women show an interest in keeping and breeding birds it appears that the Peafowl have a place in the domesticated animal structure. Their great beauty makes them fascinating subjects for study and pleasure.

SPECIAL NOTE   Much of the detail and description ap-
plies to Peafowl other than the Congo Peafowl (AFROPAVO
CONGENSIS). The latter species must be nurtured in special accommodation and is not to be recommended to those
requiring hardy birds.

Figure 1.5   The Pouter Pigeon Displaying

Figure 1.6 The Congo Peafowl (From *Peafowl of the World* –
Bergmann)

2
FEEDING
PEAFOWL

Mixed Corn (the staple diet on free range)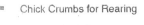

Chick Crumbs for Rearing

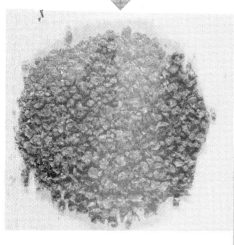

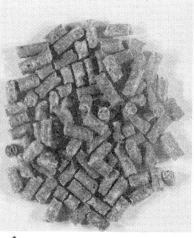

Figure 2.1 Food for Peafowl

Layers Pellets (may be fed ad lib)

FEEDING PEAFOWL

FOOD REQUIREMENTS

Free Range

The food requirements of birds can be established quite accurately. They cover the needs to grow, maintain body weight, produce feathers and, at certain times, to produce eggs.

Peafowl have similar food requirements to the domestic fowl and, therefore, fanciers are well equipped to cater for them. However, where Peafowl are allowed free access to pasture and other range many foods are picked up quite naturally so there is no need to provide extras to supply all that is necessary. In fact, they will thrive quite happily roaming around, finding most of their needs. A visitor to any zoological gardens can see the independence of Peafowl simply by watching where they go.

Simple Food Adequate

In these circumstances it is quite usual to scatter sufficient mixed corn to keep the birds fit and healthy. Around 4oz per day is a rough guide, but if birds appear very hungry give them more and, conversely, if they leave food then cut down the amount.

Semi-Intensive Feeding

Sometimes Peafowl are kept in large aviaries and then they must be fed all the essentials and possibly Layers' Pellets will be the answer. These contain all the necessary proteins, starches, fats and vitamins as well as grit so all the needs are covered.

The body size will affect the amount of food taken and since a Peafowl is around the size of a small Turkey; e.g. 20 lb, the amount of food will be similar. No statistics appear to have been compiled but around 6-8 oz per day would appear to be the norm, but the exact amount will depend on the age of the bird and the protein level of the food.

Greenstuff is essential for all types of poultry and Peafowl are no exception. Chickweed, grass clippings, leaves and other edible plants can all be fed on a regular basis. It is an established fact that a plentiful supply of green food helps to combat disease. A number of green foods contain vitamin E which is vital for reproduction.

A ZOO VISIT

A visit by the author to Blackpool Zoo showed Peafowl in all areas. However, they seemed to be attracted by the moat surrounding the elephant enclosure. This had a perimeter hedge which provided some shelter from the sun, but it also appeared to provide food because the Peafowl foraged at the bottom of the dry moat. In addition, they flew up to the concrete area where the elephants lived. Delacour *(The Pheasants of the World)* notes the belief that Peafowl associate with tigers and leopards. Could there also be an attraction to elephants or to insects or other food in the proximity of these large animals?

The natural food is really anything which takes their fancy seeds, berries, leaves, flowers, fruits, insects, worms, grass and other items growing or existing in field or garden. In essence their requirements are similar to domestic poultry. The difference lies in their semi-wild state which makes

18

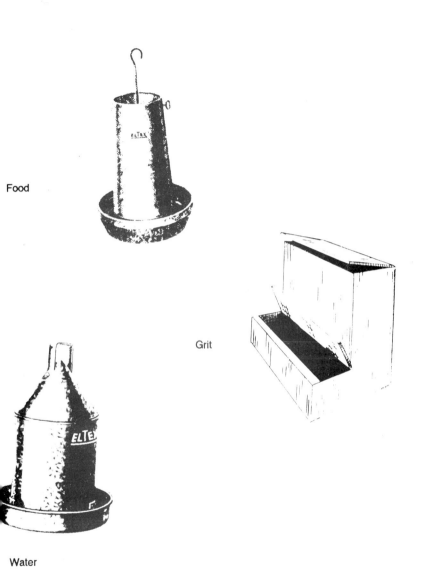

Food

Grit

Water

Figure 2.2   Feeding Hoppers and Water Fountain

them absolutely self-reliant and therefore very economic to keep. They forage morning and evening finding all their requirements. The exception is when rearing Peafowl chicks when a high protein food should be given.

Because they require to forage as a natural part of their life style Peafowl are best kept in spacious grounds such as Park-land, orchards, paddocks, woods and open spaces. They are not at home in a small garden although many do lead quite healthy lives in areas of one-quarter of an acre or above. They love to roost in trees and on garden sheds and out-houses, thus displaying themselves to full advantage.

NATURAL FOOD

Of all the grains wheat is the best, if it had to be fed alone; i.e., peafowl would do better on wheat alone than on any other grain alone. But variety is best and should be the aim.

DIFFERENT APPROACHES

There are many different possibilities for feeding all poultry. If feeding for laying there should be a mixture of protein, vitamins, minerals and fibre. Care should be taken to ensure that the level of protein is correct for the weight and productive capacity of the birds. Otherwise the extra protein will be converted into fat. Remember an overfed bird will not lay to its maximum capacity!

The approximate quantities of the main requirements are as follows:

	Percentage
Protein	15
Calcium (limestone grit)	3
Fibre	Up to 10
Vitamins A, B2, D and Folic Acid	

When birds are kept on free range with adequate sunshine there should be no problem providing adequate calcium and vitamins. Also, under the same conditions, the percentage of protein required may be reduced to 50 per cent of the suggested amount; i.e. around 7.5 per cent. When the birds are kept in a scratching shed they should be given plenty of greenstuff, and cod-liver oil should be added to the feed. A balanced diet should be the aim.

Mixing this diet can save money, but without adequate knowledge the maximum results will not be obtained. This is why in the long run it may be safer to keep to ready-mixed foods purchased from the feeding stuff manufacturer. Food can be purchased to suit the particular type of bird being kept.

AD LIB FEEDING

Keeping layers' mash, crumbs or pellets before the birds at all times ensures that they receive sufficient. This is a labour-saving practice and, surprisingly, birds do not usually over-feed. Hoppers can be purchased which hold 28 lb. or more.

If a cheaper, supplementary food is to be given, this can be in the form of wheat or mixed corn (wheat, broken maize and barley). A good plan is to scatter the grain so that the birds have to scratch for it. Late afternoon is a good time for giving this meal, allowing a handful per bird. Usually the birds look forward to receiving mixed corn even when mash is available at all times.

A further change can be given in the form of grass clippings, leaves, weeds from the garden and other digestible litter: leaves are a very neglected source of food.

POSSIBLE FOODS

Wheat, barley, maize and oats are the main food for

Peafowl. However, what is required is an additional form of protein. Fish meal, meat meal, bone meal, milk, dried yeast and other sources of protein are vital.

Foods which have been used are given below. Potatoes and potato peelings may be used as a base for a wet mash. They supply carbohydrates and, boiled until easily "mashed", provide a digestible food. If too many potatoes or other scraps are given there will be a loss of protein and vitamins.

An advantage of "wet" mash is that birds tend to eat it greedily and, therefore, is quite suitable for a booster feed on cold days. As noted later, a wet mash should not be noticeably wet; rather it should be crumbly so that the birds eat without dificulty.

DIFFERENT TYPES OF FOOD

The various forms of suitable food are given below. Stale bread (not mouldy) may also be used; soaked in water it will be found that birds will gobble it greedily. The occasional feed of bread will stimulate the appetite. However, if used as the base for a wet mash there should be additions of bran, ground oats, barley meal or other "mash"; this soaks up the surplus moisture. Meat or fish meal should be added to give the desired level of protein.

Remember though that Peafowl do not lay all the year and therefore a high protein diet is not vital all the time.

Peas and beans are rich in protein, and we may see why our most powerful horses thrive on beans, and long distance racing pigeons on peas, but the food is too concentrated for poultry, except when given as meal in small quantities, about one part in seven as a morning feed.

Oats form an almost perfect food. There is nothing like it for adding size and stamina to growing stock.

Maize is too rich in fatty matter to be fed alone, but when used alternately with oats is a first class food. There has been too great an outcry against maize. Liver diseases and other ailments have been attributed to it, which are now traced to other sources. It is rich in carbohydrates.

Grass is almost a perfect food provided it is young.

Barley, by analysis, would not appear to be over fattening, but it is, and is very hard to digest. It is one of the worst foods for fowls, and they show their distaste for it by leaving it till last when fed with a mixture of other grains. Barley Meal when finely ground is a good food when mixed with other meals.

Sharps, Pollards, or Thirds, are various names given to the same article, the refuse from wheat after the bran has been taken off when grinding for fine flour. It is on analysis about the same as wheat.

Ground Oats – Mixed with Maize Meal it is an ideal food for all kinds of fowl.

Dry Meat Meal* can be bought in various forms and is one of the most convenient of all forms for adding the required proportion of protein.

Green or Fresh Cut Bone is another, and is keenly relished both by growing stock and laying hens. It may sometimes be purchased ready for use at about the same price as Dry Meat Meal, but it does not keep wholesome for many days. It is a good thing to purchase a pressure cooker, and to arrange with the local butcher to supply the bones. The great difference in cost soon pays for the cooker.

---

* Recent outbreaks of Salmonella have suggested that meat is a doubtful food and should be used with caution.

Fish Meal, the product of dried fish, ground up bones and flesh together, is also rich in protein. An addition of about one part to twelve parts of Sharps or other Meal makes a rich food, and is especially valuable during the breeding season. It is the base of the well known "Liverine", an excellent food.

Biscuit Meal, made by many animal food supply firms, is also excellent. When used it should be placed in a pail or bucket about half filled, and boiling water poured over it and a cloth placed on the top to keep in the heat and steam. This causes it to swell. The other Meals can then be added to it in the proportion of at least one half and the whole mixed into a crumbly mass.

Bran served in the same way is a nourishing food. Unless well scalded, it is apt to cause intestinal irritation, but both chicks and adults eat it dry with safety.

MIXING FOODS

The Morning Meal should consist of soft food mixed with hot water. Several recipes are given below. The whole should be well stirred together and mixed so as to be moist and crumbly When rolled into a ball with the hand and thrown upon the grass, or placed in the trough, it should fall to pieces. So long as all the Meal is moistened it is better too dry than too sloppy. Only as much should be given to the birds as they will eat readily at once. It is better to give too little than to leave food lying about to go sour and to encourage rats, etc.

ALTERNATIVE DIETS

Peafowl naturally require more during the time they are laying, and should be given as much as they will eat, and the same when they are deep in moult. At other times they should be kept fairly hungry or they will become too fat.

POSSIBLE RECIPES

No. 1

Sharps	–	2 parts
Barley Meal	–	1 part
Meat Meal	–	1/4 part

No. 2

Maize Meal	–	2 parts
Bran (scalded)	–	1 part
Sharps	–	3 parts
Meat Meal	–	1/2 part

A NOTE ON FOOD AND VITAMINS

A fancier desires to have healthy birds and this means the correct environment and adequate food which usually means a balanced diet. As noted earlier, the essential components are as follows:

1. **Protein**
2. **Carbohydrates** (starches)
3. **Fats**
4. **Water**
5. **Calcium**

BASIC CONSTITUENTS

There are three basic constituents necessary in the diet of all living creatures; namely, **proteins**, **carbohydrates** and **fats**. These three elements mustbe contained in any given diet, and what is more important , they must be balanced against each other if all of the dietary requirementsof the birds are to be met.

25

A plentiful supply of water is vital. Without it the birds will lose weight. Stating exact quantities is difficult because of the moisture which is in greenstuff. However, in warm weather a Peafowl is likely to require between one and two litres of liquid per day.

Protein

It is frequently, and perhaps correctly, argued that protein is the most essential constituent in the diet of any type of animal life. Protein is the substance which builds the muscles and which will quite literally put the meat on the bones.

Carbohydrates

Another essential part of the diet is the carbohydrate content. This is the dietary element which gives energy and which is used up rapidly by the body processes, especially when exercise is being taken, rather in the same way as coal is consumed in a fire.

Fats within Food

Fats are another important part of the diet. These elements supplement the carbohydrates and also generate body heat.

From this information, it can clearly be seen that the emphasis on a balanced diet cannot be stressed too strongly. What, for example, is the point in giving a diet which is overloaded with protein, if the carbohydrates are insufficient to burn up the excess proteins? In such a case, the result would be obesity in the stock rather than a balanced type of bird. Pieces of fat are not recommended.

SPECIAL NOTES

1. Growing feathers, beaks, toenails require **an extra amount of protein** and, therefore, young birds should be given a special diet containing a high level of protein.

2. **Amino Acids** are essential for growth and, therefore, must be present in the diet. A variety of food is essential for the bird to achieve the level of amino acids it requires.

3. **Vitamins** These are essential to the well being of Peafowl. They are:

(a) **Vitamin A** – Fish liver oil is the best source, but greens and carrots are also essential and are taken readily. A deficiency will result in poor breeding results, constant colds (breathing difficulties), watery eyes and thick mucous around the nostrils. Cod-liver oil should be mixed with the corn and the wild greens listed later. In addition, lettuce, spinach, kale and other fresh greens should be given. Bleached vegetables should not be given. Cabbage or brussel sprouts do not give a high level of vitamin A. Grass meal and yellow maize are natural sources of Vitamin A.

(b) **Vitamin D** – Lack of vitamin D results in leg, joint, beak and other bone growth problems (rickets). Adding cod liver oil and feeding calcium in some form will help to combat the deficiency, but sunshine is the essential requirement. The ultra violet rays from the sun are vital and special lamps can provide rays, but may damage the eyes of the birds due to being too strong. Sunshine through clean glass is not helpful because the ultra violet rays may not pass through.

(c) **Vitamin E** – This vitamin provides the necessary component for reproduction. Its main source is sprouting seeds such as wheat and certain leaf plants such as lettuce, watercress and spinach. Egg yolk is also a prime source. However, wheatgerm oil should be mixed separately from cod–liver oil, although the two can be used on seed provided they are mixed separately.

(d) **Vitamin K** – This is essential to avoid haemorrhages on breast, wings and legs. It is found in grass.

TURKEY RATIONS = PEAFOWL RATIONS

Because of its body size the Peafowl comes nearest to the Turkey and, therefore, for those fanciers who wish to minimize on labour and feed ad lib, using hoppers, may use turkey rations. These will make use of natural foods such as maize, wheat, barley, fish, soya beans, grass meal as well as vitamins, limestone flour and other additives.

Usually recognition is given to the following stages of growth, with separate foods (starters' pellets, rearers' pellets, etc.):

1. **Starter** – fed from 2 days to around 5 weeks. It contains about 27 per cent protein. Ideally it should also include drugs to prevent coccidiosis and blackhead, both serious diseases.

2. **Rearer** – follows on from the **starter** and contains around 23 per cent protein. For a few days the birds should be given both types of food and thereafter switched to Rearers only. The anti–blackhead should be continued and any signs of drooping wings and uneven feather growth will probably mean the birds have contracted coccidiosis. If this occurs then a coccidiostat should be put in the water thus combatting the disease.

3. **Layers\Breeders** – this should be fed from January onwards and continued throughout the breeding season. It will contain about 18 per cent protein. At this stage if wheat has been fed (with the Rearers) this should be cut out.

If birds have access to an outside paddock or orchard the Breeders ration can be limited, making up the difference with mixed corn and what the Peafowl can forage.

A summary of the constituents of the turkey rations described is given below:

BREAK–DOWN PEAFOWL/TURKEY RATIONS

Constituents	Starter	Rearer	Breeder
Maize meal	30	20.75	20
Wheat meal	16.25	27	39
Barley meal	10	20	10
Fish meal	14	8	7
Soya bean meal	20	12	11
Grass meal	5	5	5
D.D.S.	2.50	2.50	3.50
Synthetic vitamins*	1	0.75	1
Limestone flour	–	1.50	2
D.C.P.	1	2	1
Salt	0.25	0.50	0.50
	100	100	100

* The vitamin and trace element requirements are very high and should be met through the provision of a special proprietary turkey supplement.

AMPLE FOOD ESSENTIAL

Peafowl should not be deprived of access to a plentiful supply of food. In winter, when natural food is in short supply, mixed corn should be scattered in a barn or deep litter shed so they can exercise and at the same time obtain adequate food for withstanding the cold. They are hardy birds, quite able to withstand the rigours of the harshest winter, but food and shelter are vital.

A MORE BASIC RATION

Some breeders prefer to use a lower protein diet even when Peafowl are kept semi-intensive. In such cases a basic poultry ration will suffice:

1. LAYERS' PELLETS – for adult birds

2. GROWERS' PELLETS – for young stock around 6 weeks and upwards.

3. CHICK CRUMBS – for day old to 3-4 weeks gradually changing to Growers Pellets and chopped corn. Regular greens such as chickweed and grass clippings should also be given. This supplementary food appears to help chicks over the period when they are feathering and helps to combat disease.

Some breeders advocate using chick crumbs for as long a period as 8 weeks, but this is rather a long time on a "baby ration" and the author believes that growth is more natural if other foods are introduced as early as possible. Bread soaked in milk or water may be taken quite readily by the growing birds and seems to stimulate the appetite.

3

ANATOMY

Spur of Green Peafowl

KEEPING PEAFOWL

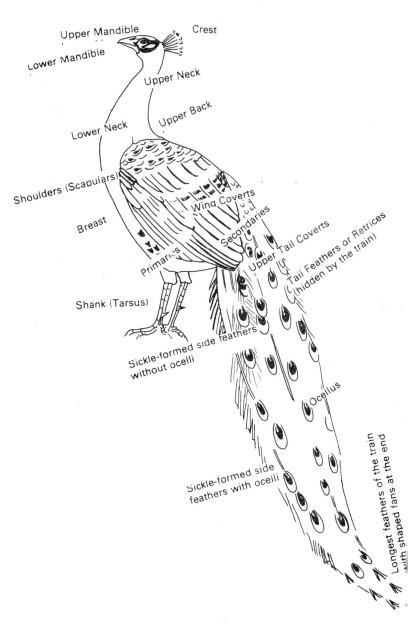

3.1 Main Features of the Peafowl

ANATOMY OF THE PEAFOWL

OVERALL SIZE

The Peafowl are large birds; their sizes are approximately as follows:

INDIAN (BLUE) PEAFOWL *(Pavo cristatus)*
in millimetres

	Male	Female
Length	2100	1000
Wing	470	420
Tail	1500	360
Culmen	42	38
Tarsus	150	125
(Shank of Leg)		

GREEN PEAFOWL *(Pavo muticus)*

	Male	Female
Length	2400	1000
Wing	500	430
Tail	1500	425
Culmen	43	41
Tarsus	165	140

In these true Peafowl we have extremely large species of bird. An average measurement has been taken   based on the data given by Delacour and others. It will be seen that

Figure 3.2 Peahen's Nest in a Tree
The Peafowl is basically a semi-wild bird so close confinement is not advisable

KEEPING PEAFOWL

the *Pavo muticus* is a larger bird and it also tends to be more vigorous and possibly wilder in nature. It will be seen that the male birds are over 7 ft long including the tail, which is around 4.5 ft. Females are smaller being around 3 ft long in body with a relatively short tail.

CONGO PEAFOWL *(Afropavo)*
millimetres

	Male	Female
Length	660	610
Wing	320	280
Tail	240	210
Culmen	33	31
Tarsus	101	87

In appearance the Congo Peafowl male and female are similar in size with only a slight difference in the length of the tail.

As indicated earlier, these are delicate birds in captivity and strictly should not be thought of in the same terms as the better known species *cristatus* and *muticus*. They are not easy to keep or rear so are limited in scope for the amateur aviculturist.

THE ANATOMY

The anatomy of the Peafowl follows that of other poultry and functions in a similar way. It may be viewed from two aspects:

1. The internal organs responsible for providing suste-nance and the means of developing eggs in the female bird.

35

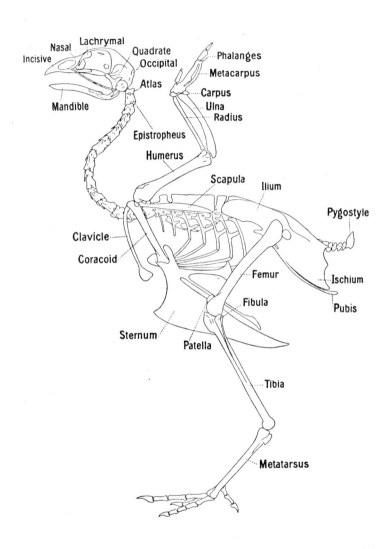

Figure 3.3 Skeleton of Gallinaceous Bird

2. The external shape and characteristics.

An understanding of both is vital. The provision of appro-priate food, water and minerals is vital to success. Unsuitable foods do not provide the essentials and can lead to health problems. For chicks higher protein food develops bone, flesh and feathers and ensures rapid growth. The outward shape, including the face, beak, crest, neck, body, legs, wings and feathers show the species of bird. The external shape and appearance indicate important facts on the type of bird.

THE SKELETON AND INTERNAL ORGANS
The internal organs of a bird fit within a structure of bones the skeleton (Figure 3.3). A summary of the principal parts is:

1. Breast bone
The breastbone or sternum is a vital part of the body. It protects the internal organs as well as a foundation for the flesh and muscles which operate the wings.

2. Wings
The wings provide the means of flying. Their positioning is of vital importance in determining style and posture; when carried high the thighs are revealed and the result is a taller looking bird.

3. Legs and Feet
The legs and feet provide the means of walking, and perching. They should be free from bumps or enlarged scales.

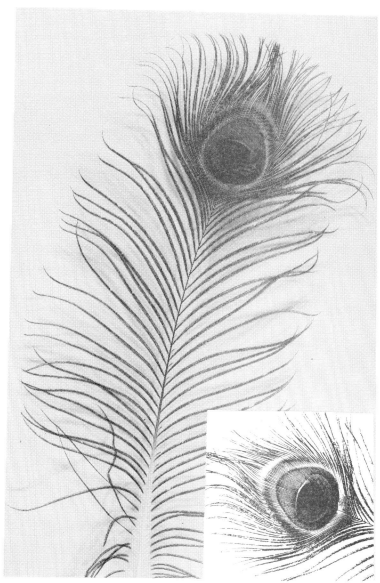

Figure 3.4 Tail feathers from Peacock

Peafowl have quite long legs which give them a rather majestic appearance.

4. Head

The head is mounted upon the neck which is quite flexible. At the front of the skull is the beak made up of the upper and lower mandible. Size and shape of head is of vital importance.

PHYSIOLOGY

The functioning of the bird is relatively simple and yet is an incredible process. Food is converted into flesh and\or eggs which, after incubation become chicks which rapidly grow into adult birds, and then at about three years of age they too become producers, thus repeating the process. The main parts are as follows:

1. Beak

Food is picked up by a bird and proceeds down the throat into the **crop**, a bag made of skin, and from there it goes on to the **gizzard**.

2. Crop and Gizzard

The crop is the store for food just taken and this passes into a passageway known as a proventriculis (or ventriculus) before passing into the gizzard. The latter is an almost solid organ which masticates food so that it can be digested.

3. Intestines

From the gizzard food passes into the intestines and after due processing is passed out through the rectum (or vent).

Within the digestive framework there are:

(a) **Liver** in which is found the gall bladder which stores the bile;
(b) **Kidneys** (two) which filter the liquids and excrete uric acid.

Blood and Air Circulation

The blood is circulated by the contraction and expansion of the heart which is usually likened to a pump which has four chambers – the upper two ,named "auricles" and the lower two the "ventricles".

The bird breathes through its nostrils or mouth into the bronchial tubes and lungs. The arterial veins from the heart pass through the lungs thus allowing the circulating blood to be oxygenated.

REPRODUCTIVE SYSTEM

For successful reproduction both male and female should be in good health and well fed. Eggs should become fertile within a few days of male and female being placed together, but generally a period of ten days is considered to be a safe waiting time.

The female has two ovaries only one of which usually develops. In addition, there is the oviduct a long twisting tube consisting of two parts through which a yolk passes, adding the various parts ("white", membranes and shell) until the egg falls into the cloaca or egg pouch.

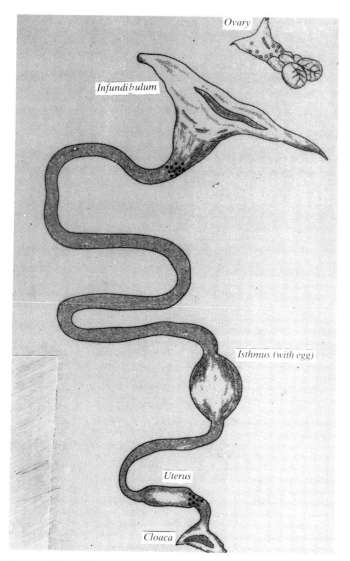

Figure 3.5   The Reproductive System

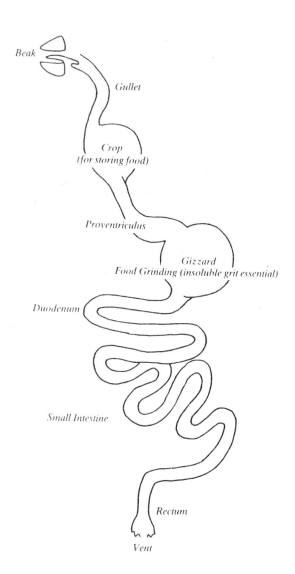

Figure 3.6 The Digestive System

Opinions on how long the process takes vary, but generally around eighteen hours is regarded as the cycle time.
Within the ovary there are many embryo eggs (oocytes) –
more than 1500 have been counted in a fowl's ovary. These
develop so that a few large yolks ripen (usually about five)
until one is ready to go into the oviduct for development
into the egg.

The male bird "treads" the hen and thereby fertilises the
eggs. He discharges semen from testes into two ducts and
thence into the oviduct of the female when the mating takes
place.

THE EGG

Creating Egg Colour

The actual colour comes from glands in the oviduct and is
transferred by pigments:

(a) oocyanin – Basal Blue
(b) ooclilomin – Yellow
(c) ooxanthin – Red or Purplish
(d) ooporphrin – pattern forming

This colouring stage takes place in the lower part of the
oviduct known   as the uterus and it is at this point that a
coating of calcium carbonate is coated over the shell membrane.

The Peafowl egg is not highly coloured, but tends to be
of a creamy colour, occasionally having spots.

The Shell – General Notes

The Outer shell of the egg is made up of three distinct

layers:

1. **Cuticle** – a fine coating which gives the egg its lustre or bloom.
2. **Palisade or spongy Layer** – the bulk of the shell (approx. 2/3 of the thickness).
3. **Mammillary** – the INNER part.

The shell is very strong and relative to its size can withstand great pressure. (Peahen 10 kilobreaking strength – weight approximately 95 gramme. Hen egg 60 gramme 4.1 kilos breaking strength, whereas a small fresh egg, 1 gramme in weight, will withstand 0.1 kilo.

Creating the Shell

The top-quality shell comes from the healthy bird, managed in a suitable environment with the appropriate type of food, water and other essentials.

Birds flying out of doors with access to grass, vegetation earth and other natural objects usually produce eggs of good quality. The calcium carbonate required to produce the shell comes from the food eaten and from sand, stones, leaves and other small items picked up. Limestone is the main ingredient for the shell substance and yet nowhere will it be obviously available.

Proper functioning requires the quantity absorbed to be considered and must be consumed by each hen according to her requirements. Birds kept in aviaries, may be given fine oyster shell and limestone provided in suitable hoppers. If topped up regularly the hens will regulate their own consumption.

Birds in the wild eat grit each day. Ornithologists have found that game birds consume considerable quantities of grit even though they may lay only around 30 eggs per season. Obviously, though, egg production is not the only required consideration. Adequate nutrition requires an efficient digestive system and this depends upon the functioning of the gizzard. This will function without insoluble grit, but is much more effective when birds are able to eat as much grit as required.

Pheasants, doves, partridges, geese and other birds have been observed taking their daily intake of gravel or other grit.

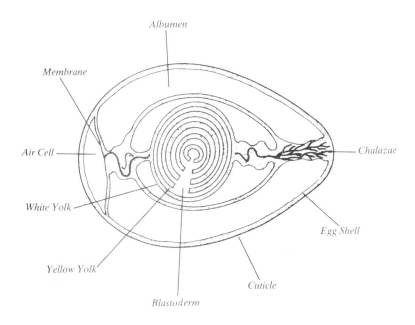

Figure 3.7   The Egg

Note: Terms are self explanatory except the CHALAZAE which is a special part of the albumen

45

Research Findings

Percentages found in the crops of pheasant was 26 per cent and in Hungarian partridge it was 40 per cent. These were much higher than for grouse (6 per cent) and Mallard (13 per cent). They were not regarded as conclusive evidence of the normal intake percentages, but rather they confirm the need for regular supplies of grit.

SIZE OF GRIT

When grit is fed to birds it should be appropriate to the size of bird. Birds such as grouse or pheasant should be supplied with small granules which then can consume easily in their gizzards should the supply be cut off. Smaller birds should be given grit which is rather like coarse sand.

It will be appreciated that two types of grit are essential; flint for grinding foods and soluble grit for egg shells.

THE MEMBRANE

Within the shell there are two membranes:

1. **Inner Membrane** which surrounds the albumen.
2. **Outer Membrane** which adheres to the inside of the outer membrane except at the broad end occupied by the air space.

Air Space

The air space is non-existent in a new laid egg, but gradually appears, taking as little as two minutes (or longer), depending upon the rate at which the egg cools. It supplies a vital air supply to the chicks and without it they would die.

4

HOUSING PEAFOWL

Figure 4.1 A Typical Shed and Aviary

HOUSING PEAFOWL

AMPLE SIZE ESSENTIAL

The Peafowl is a very large bird and, therefore, should be housed in accommodation which is appropriate to its size. A normal poultry shed and run will almost certainly be inadequate. How can the Peacock, with its large, fan tail avoid frustration and damage unless it has enough space to turn around? Ideally Peafowl should be kept in a barn or large shed with a perch well off the ground; e.g. 2 metres for the cock and 1.2 metres for the hen. It is important to allow for the tail which will touch the ground and get soiled if too low. On the other hand, if too high a bird may injure itself or may have difficulty in getting up on to the perch or back down on to the ground. Some form of stepped system of perches might be adopted provided the housing is wide enough inside.

Perches should be wide enough to support the bird correctly, enabling it to wrap its toes around. With all types of poultry the natural shape for a perch is for it to be rounded, preferably oval for this allows a better grip and balance. However, the Peafowl appears to show no preference for any type of perch.

Peacocks have been seen to perch in trees, on the top of sheds or other buildings, on chimneys and any other convenient edifice. Accordingly, it would seem that they are prepared to accept any reasonable management. With any domestic poultry intended for exhibition care must be taken with perches to avoid duckfootedness, but this does not apply to Peafowl which are not usually entered in shows.

Peafowl are not really flying birds and usually get out of difficulties by running. They are active birds not taking kindly to restrictions. If successful breeding is sought the outdoor run should be quite large. The numbers to keep depend on circumstances but usually in an aviary a single pair will be adequate. Outdoors a cock will produce fertile eggs with three or four hens.

THE AVIARY AND RUN
General

The aviary is intended to keep birds in captivity, but in such a way that they enjoy life and show this fact by breeding and reacting in a normal way with song or other characteristic behaviour.

Peafowl have to be given a large aviary at least 4 metres high and around 8 metres square thus giving plenty of room for turning and for perching.

In addition, there should be quarters for sleeping or for keeping indoors when the weather is quite inclement. Peafowl prefer plenty of fresh air so an open-fronted house will be preferred (with bars or wire netting). However, there should be sufficient overlap on the roof to allow adequate shelter from rain and wind.

Wire Netting

There is no hard and fast rule on the size of wire netting to use. For economy 1" (25mm) is to be recommended but use a good strong gauge or it will be false economy. Poor quality wire netting rusts very quickly and foxes and dogs will find a way in.

An alternative to netting is "twilweld" a mesh made of

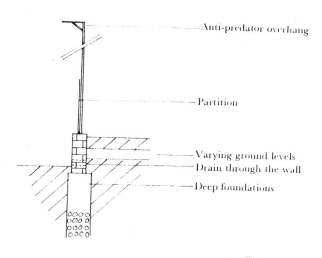

Fig 4.2   Aviary Plan to show safety precautions against predators

galvanised wire made of squares. This is quite stron
and easy to handle, but tends to be more expensive tha
the conventional wire netting.

Wind Breakers

The problems encountered with a completely wire
netted run are considerable. There is little or no shelter, th
birds are easily startled by fox, dog or other marauder an
access is more easil effected.

A better idea is to erect wind-breakers made of stron
boards or corrugated sheets. These may be painted blac
or green to make the run look attractive. Alternatively, one c
the newer materials such as moulded plastic can be used, bu
these are not as strong as corrugated sheets. Possibly the
would be more appropriate for covering the roof the ru
and aviary house for they maximise the light.

THE FLOOR

Opinions differ on what is the most appropriate materia
to use for the floor of the house and aviary. Possibilitie
are as follows:

House

1. Boards
2. Concrete or Pebbles
3. Earth/Sand/Leaves, etc.
4. Flagstones
5. Wire mesh raised from the ground
6. Slats raised from the ground

Run

All the above could also be used for the run, but in practical terms either a concrete or pebble surface or a natural earth run, will be the most appropriate. The concrete or pebbles can be washed down using a hose and are, therefore, hygienic. Unfortunately, they are cold and unimaginative. The birds have nothing to occupy themselves so they become bored and resort to bad habits such as feather pecking. In their favour they can be kept clean and thereby avoid disease such as coccidiosis and worm infestations. Moreover, turf, grass clippings, weeds, leaves and other natural food can be thrown into the run thereby supplementing the food and giving the birds something to do.

Earth Floor

With the earth floor care must be taken to ensure that it does not become stale and water logged. Various sugges- tions can be made:

(a) Dig over at regular intervals (only partially successful)

(b) Add new soil, leaves, clippings, peat moss and sand to build up the level. This can be done on a regular basis from the garden and works extremely well.

(c) Add lime or suitable sterilising agent to the soil at the end of each year, preferably digging in and giving the ground a rest for a few weeks.

The experience of the author favours (b) above.

Obviously much depends upon circumstances. If plenty of material is available such as lawn clippings, weeds or leaves they will provide all that is necessary. However, if there is a shortage of natural food, green stuff such as chickweed, docks, groundsel ,as well as apples, should be given.

SITE OF AVIARY

Care should be taken in selecting a site for an aviary. Peafowl are large birds and the position selected will affect their health and productivity. Factors to consider are:

1. **Size** Since a large aviary is essential the site should be large enough to take the closed shelter and the aviary. If birds are also to be given a certain amount of freedom the outside should be suitable for peafowl to forage.

2. **Shelter** Adequate protection from winds and sleet and snow is vital, yet if placed in too low a position frost may linger and cause pneumonia. Wind breakers and possibly some form of roof covering may also be advisable.

3. **Well-Drained Aviary** Muddy, water-logged conditions are quite unsuitable for all peafowl. Accordingly if not on well-drained soil the bottom of the aviary should be built up. In extreme cases drains will have to be installed thus ensuring that adequate drainage is maintained.

4. **Sunny Aspect** A bright, sunny aspect is essential and therefore select a site which allows as much sun as possible, but with adequate shelter such as an overhanging tree for when the birds wish to rest.

5. **Optimum Position** Select a spot which is convenient for access with a pathway leading to it for watering and feeding. Ensure that the birds can be protected from predators.

Fig 4.3 Typical Perching Arrangement with droppings board

6. Landscape Try to make the aviary as attractive as possible. Instead of corrugated sheets as wind breakers consider an evergreen hedge such as laurel. Ideally the natural habitat of the peafowl should be the aim, but this is not always feasible or practicable.

SIZE OF AVIARY

Considering the length of the Peacock is over 7 feet (around 2 metres) it will be apparent that adequate turning space will require at least 3 metres in width, preferably 4 metres. Nothing is worse for captive birds to be cramped in small aviaries with little or nothing to do. If Peafowl are observed it will be noted that they are active birds, foraging and darting from one place to another. They have to be able to move around and perch without damaging feathers particularly the tail.

The fully developed tail is over a metre in length and therefore perches should be at a level which gives adequate clearance from the ground. A stepping system is probably the best approach with an intermediate perch or shelf to give a jumping off position for the birds. Allowing for at least a metre for the tail, it follows that the final roosting perch should be about 2 metres from the floor of the shed or aviary.

Aviary Layout

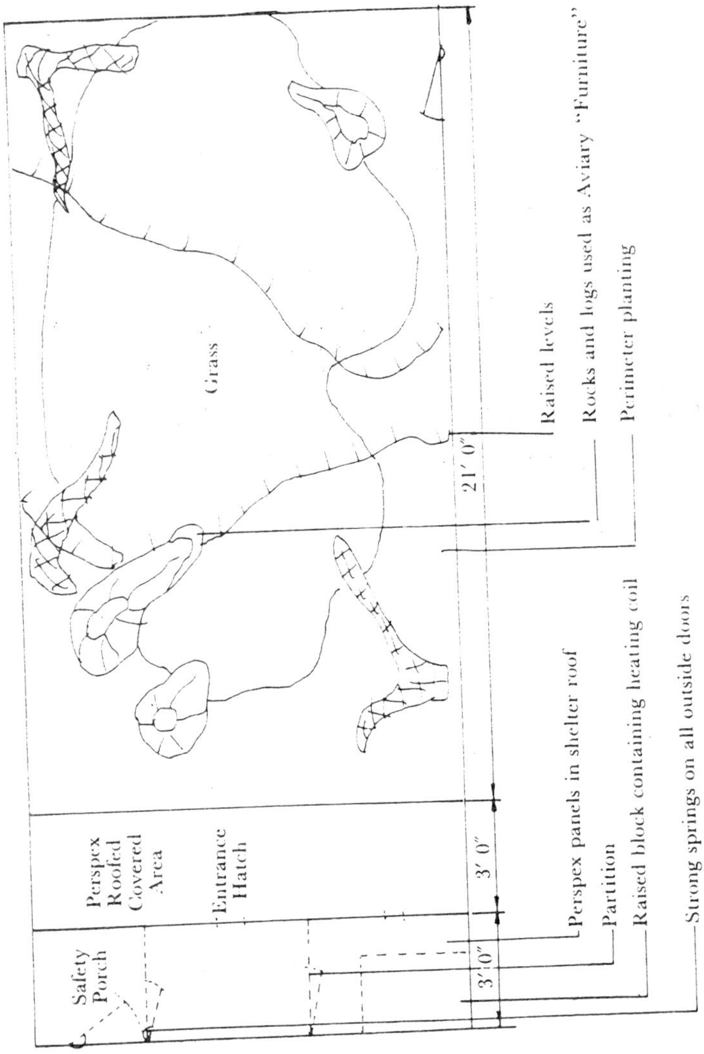

Safety Porch

Perspex Roofed Covered Area

Entrance Hatch

Grass

3' 0"

3' 0"

21' 0"

Perspex panels in shelter roof

Partition

Raised block containing heating coil

Strong springs on all outside doors

Raised levels

Rocks and logs used as Aviary "Furniture"

Perimeter planting

Figure 4.6 Landscaping an Aviary

5

BREEDING

Figure 5.0 Portable brooder with run for younger birds

Fig 5.1 The Broody Hen on Her Nest

BREEDING

INCUBATION

There are two methods:

1. Natural Incubation:
   (a) Peahen
   (b) Surrogate mother such as a broody hen

2. Artificial Incubation using an incubator.

NATURAL INCUBATION

A background knowledge of how the birds behave in the wild is useful to understand what is required. If natural conditions can be copied there is a good chance of success.

In the wild state Peafowl nest at different times depending upon the area, the climate and availability of food; in a dry season no insects would be available so trying to breed would be a waste of time.

Nesting takes place in a variety of places:

(a) Foot of bushes on hill sides, relying on the fallen leaves for camoflage
(b) Top of low bushes
(c) In branches of tall trees or buildings particularly when flooding occurs.

The Nest

Sometimes the Peahen will scratch a hole and place

twigs or leaves to , for m a nest. At other times the eggs are laid in a natural hollow.

The Egg*

This is quite substantial in size and has a thick shell. Various authors have described them and their comments are reproduced below:

Typical Rasorial ones, much like gigantic guinea-fowl's eggs, with thick, very strong and glossy shells, closely pitted over their whole surface with minute pores. (Hume)

In colour they vary from a very pale cream or fawn to a warm buff or cafe-au-lait, the majority being a rather decided, though pale, buff or cream. Occasionally one comes across eggs which are freckled with a colour the same as, but darker than, the ground colour and I have one egg in my collection which is mottled all over with a dull grey which makes the egg look as if mildewed.

Hume also mentions eggs freckled with reddish brown as thickly as those of the Monal, but such eggs are very exceptional. In shape the eggs are broad blunt ovals, with both ends almost the same, though they vary a good deal, whilst I have seen one abnormal clutch of eggs almost as peg-top-shaped as a Plover's.

I have no eggs bigger than the biggest in the Hume collection, which measure 3 inches (= 76.2 mm.) in length, and 2.2 inches (= 55.8 mm.) in breadth, but I have a remarkable clutch from the Khasia Hills of which the five eggs average only 2.5 inches (= 63.5 mm.) x 1.8 inches (= 45.7 mm.), and of which the smallest is only 2.45 inches (= 62.2 mm.) x 1.42 inches (= 35.7 mm.).

*Whether to clean and/or sterilise the shells of the eggs should be considered (see end of chapter.)

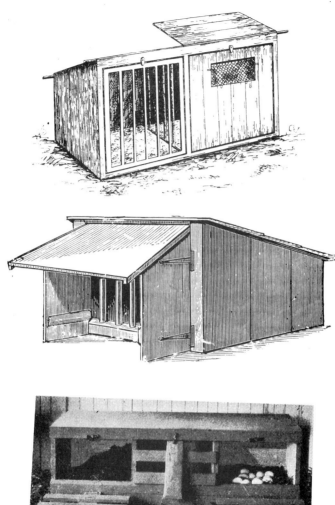

Figure 5.2   Broody Coops

Eighty eggs average 69.5 x 52.0 mm.; maxima 76.2 x 54.1 and 73.4 x 58.9 mm.; minima 61.2 x 43.1 mm. (Baker)
In fact, as shown, the size varies tremendously. Around 68mm x 50 mm wide is the norm with a weight of 90-95 grammes.

INCUBATION PERIOD

Baker cites 32 to 35 days for incubation in England but shorter in India. In fact around 28-30 days is the correct period with 26 days for the Congo Peafowl.

MATING

The Peacock is noted for his proud strutting and fantastic display. Unfortunately, once the cock "treads" the hen, in the same manner as other poultry*, he loses interest and is not involved in incubation or rearing the chicks. In fact, he should be kept away from the whole process or he may inflict damage to eggs or chicks.

A background to the whole process of preparing for reproduction may be seen from the quotation below:

In the months of December and January the temperature in the forests of Central India, especially in the valleys, is very low, and the cold, from sudden evaporation, intense at sunrise. The Peafowl in the forests may be observed at such times still roosting, long after the sun has risen above the horizon. As the mist rises off the valleys, and gathering into little clouds, goes rollling up the hill-sides till lost in the ethereal blue, the Peafowl descend from their perch on some huge simal or sal tree, and, threading their way in

---

**This is only partially true. I have kept a number of Old English Game cocks who would look after the chicks allowing them to go underneath at night..

silence through the underwood, emerge into the fields, and make sad havoc with the channa, urad (both vetches), wheat, or rice. When sated, they retire into the neighbouring thin jungle, and there preen themselves, and dry their bedewed plumage in the sun. The cock stands on a mound, or a fallen trunk, and sends forth his well-known cry, "pehaun-pehaun", which is soon answered from other parts of the forest. The hens ramble about, or lie down dusting their plumage, and so they pass the early hours while the air is still cool, and hundreds of little birds are flitting and chirruping about the scarlet blossoms of the "palas" or the "simal". As the sun rises, and the dewy sparkle on the foliage dries up, the air becomes hot and still, the feathered songsters vanish into shady nooks, and our friends, the Peafowl, depart silently into the coolest depths of the forest, to some little sandy stream canopied by verdant boughs, or to thick beds of reeds and grass, or dense thorny brakes overshadowed by mossy rocks, where, though the sun blaze over the open country, the green shades are cool, and the silence of repose unbroken, though the shrill cry of the cicada may be heard ringing faintly through the wood.

These birds cease to congregate soon after the crops are off the ground. The pairing season is in the early part of the hot weather. The Peacock has then assumed his full train, that is, the longest or last rows of his upper tail-coverts, which he displays of a morning, strutting about before his wives. These strange gestures, which the natives gravely denominate the Peacock's nautch, or dance, are very similar to those of a turkey-cock, and accompanied by an occasional odd shiver of the quills, produced apparently by a convulsive jerk of the abdomen.

The same thing occurs in a turkey–cock – a little start and a puff and a short run forward, as if something had exploded unpleasantly close behind him. These are all , we are told, to allure the female, and doubtless have a most fascinating effect.

This remarkable display is well known. The Peacock excels in performance although, as noted earlier, other birds display as a preliminary to copulation.

In the wild the Peacock has an harem of four or five wives and this number can be included in a breeding pen.

NUMBER OF EGGS

Two clutches of eggs may be produced in a year. Opinions differ on the number laid in each clutch; it may vary from four eggs up to fifteen, although the norm is about six.

BREEDING TIME

From March onwards is the normal time for the Peafowl to start laying. A further clutch may be laid in May or June.

THE CLUTCH

Since the Peahen is rather unpredictable in where she will lay it follows that a careful watch must be kept on her activities. If completely free she will lay under a hedge or a hay stack or other place of concealment. In an aviary the eggs may be laid in a large nest box or on the floor.

If more than one hen is kept with the cock a communal nest may be the result. Accordingly, a mixture of eggs will be found in the one place. These should be collected and placed in a cool place for not more than 10 days. They should be marked with the date and kept in a box containing sawdust or shavings and turned each day.

If the hen Peafowl is to be encouraged to come broody artificial eggs may be placed in the nest. When a large domestic hen such as a Rhode Island or Plymouth Rock is to be used make sure she is broody, place her in a hatching coop and then release her every day for food and water. The procedure is quite simple, but remember Peafowl eggs are very large and putting too many under a hen will only diminish the chance of success. If one is not covered all the others will be affected as the eggs are turned. Remember to select a mature hen which is a proven broody; 28 days is quite a long period to sit, so a flighty pullet is likely to be unsuitable.

BROODY HENS

Nature has implanted in the heart of the hen a strong desire to perpetuate her race by sitting upon the eggs she has laid. How this desire has been eliminated from the non-sitting breeds is not known. Even these breeds show an occasional desire to sit, though they are not to be trusted with eggs, as the desire usually passes away before the incubating period of 28 days has passed.

When a hen shows the well-known signs of broodiness and it is decided to use her for sitting, it is prudent to let her sit for a day or two in the nest box normally used to make sure that the fever will not pass away. A sitting box should, in the meantime, be got ready. I find it best to have the boxes either single or in pairs, so that they can easily be moved for the purpose of cleansing.

An ideal sitting box I have found, after many experiments, is made of boards nailed together 32 in. long, 15 in. wide and 15 in. high, with a sloping top to carry off the wet. When the space occupied by the two ends and the central division is taken off, this leaves each nest a square of 15 in*. There is no wooden bottom to this box, but it is covered with a 1/2 in. wire-netting to prevent rats from burrowing, and it is placed upon the bare soil in a shady place in a small shed is ideal, away from other birds. A spadeful of earth riddled free from stones is placed in the bottom to form a depth of 2 in. of soil in the centre and more on the sites. It is formed so as to slope gently towards the centre, which is about 1 in. lower than the sides. It should be beaten down well with the hand, and made round in shape, and covered with about an inch in depth of soft meadow hay. Broken bracken also forms an ideal covering, and has the virtue of keeping away the fleas. This should be covered lightly with hay. More of this is required in cold than in warm weather. There is a door in the front to keep the hen on her nest, but at least an inch of open space should be left at the top of the entire length of the box, to admit plenty of fresh air. If the box is too tightly closed, good results are not obtained. The hen should be moved from the laying house, and placed gently on her nest with a few stale eggs under her and allowed to settle down before eggs intended to hatch are placed under her, which I prefer to do in the evening, though a good hen will take them any time of the day.

The number of eggs a hen will take depends upon her size and also the time of year. Probably four are enough for a small hen, or for cold and frosty weather, while six may be given in warm weather to a large sized hen. If more are given than a hen can comfortably cover, the outer eggs get chilled, and, as she moves them from one position to another during her period of hatching, they may all get chilled. The critical time is from about the third to the sixth day, when the germ is weak.

* This refers to a domestic fowl. A Peafowl will require a larger nestbox; around 2 x 2 x 2ft.

KEEPING PEAFOWL

The door should be opened each day at a regular hour and the hen allowed to come off for food. If she shows no disposition to leave of her own accord, she should be gently lifted off, the hands being placed under her wings and care taken that no eggs are taken out with her.

The best food is hard grain and maize may be freely used, Water should be allowed for her to drink, and a dust bath provided. A small wooden box turned on its side with a strip if wood 3 ins in depth nailed across the bottom to keep in the dry earth makes a capital bath. She is thus able to cleanse herself when necessary. The eggs take 28 days to incubate, though if the eggs are not stale and the hen is a good sitter, they frequently hatch a day early. A great deal depends on the weather. If the east winds are prevalent, the hatch is often delayed until the twenty-ninth day.

CHOICE OF BROODY HEN

The surrogate mother should be selected very carefully

(a) 28 days to sit (longer than the normal 21 days)
(b) Peafowl eggs are quite scarce, and, therefore, expensive because the Peahen will lay between 12 and 20 eggs per year as a maximum.

Accordingly, she should be healthy, free from mites, a proven sitter and mother.

Because the eggs are large the so-called "hot hen" is usually recommended. One with a full breast which covers the eggs in a thorough manner is the aim.

Light Sussex

Plymouth Rock

Figure 5.4   Broody Hens suitable for Peafowl Eggs

EXAMPLES OF BREEDS
Sitters

Aseel	Game, Indian	Orpington*
Barnevelder*	Game, Sumatra	Rock*
Brahma	Jersey Black Giant	Rhode I. Red*
Cochin	Langshan, Croad	Scots Dumpy
Dorking*	Langshan, Modern	Silkie
Faverolles	Malay	Sussex*
Game, O.E	Malines	Wyandotte*
Game, Modern	Orloff	Yokohama

*Recommended as sitters.

Non-Sitters

WHITE-SHELLED EGGS – Light or non-sitting varieties are termed "white-egg" breeds because they lay white-shelled eggs. They include:

Ancona	Houdan	Polish
Andalusian	La Bresse	Redcap
Campine	La Fleche	Scots Grey
Creve Coeur	Leghorn	Sicilian Buttercup
Hamburg	Minorca	Spanish

Often Silkie crosses are used, but the size is never very great so although admirable broodies they do not cover many eggs.

71

DIAGRAM SHOWING CORRECT AMOUNT OF AIR SPACE VISIBLE AT (OR ABOUT) 8th, 18th AND 26th DAYS

Figure 5.5   Development of the Embryo

It is better to test the eggs, from the sixth to the nin t h day, to see if they are fertile. If they are removed, in a box with a little hay on the bottom, to a dark room, in the day time or by night, and held between the thumb and finger of both hands before a strong light, e.g. a strong torch, a little practice will enable anyone to tell which have chickens in and which are clear. An unfertile egg is as clear as a new laid one, and it is well for the novice to take one of the latter as a test. The egg should be lifted with the top side as it lies in the box still uppermost, as the chick always lies at the top of the egg to be near to the warmth of the hen's body.

On the sixth or seventh day the top of the egg for about one-third of its depth will be darker than the lower portion , and a dark speck, which is the eye of the chick, can be plainly seen. At the broad end of the egg will be the air space which is empty. If there is a dark room handy, this should be done while the hen is off for her daily meal. In any case, the eggs should not be kept away more than a few minutes, and not allowed to get cool. A great deal of disappointment is often saved in this way, as well as much loss of time. Where many eggs are unfertile, e.g., where half the eggs are clear, as often happens in the season, the eggs from two hens can be placed under one and the other hen started afresh. Remember the shells of Peafowl eggs are quite thick so a strong light is essential.

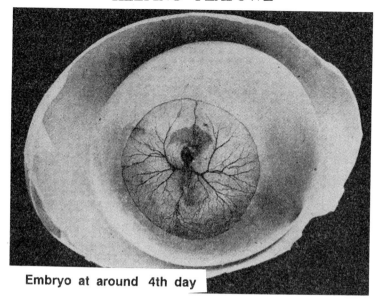

Embryo at around 4th day

DAYS

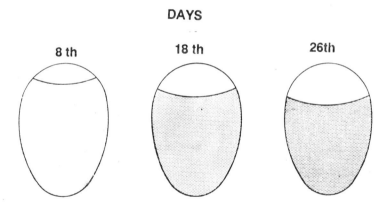

| 8 th | 18 th | 26th |

*Diagram to show correct amount of air space visible
at the periods shown*

Figure 5.5 Development of the Embryo (these are a rough guide but the
principle is very important: If gap too wide the chicks may not hatch)

DEVELOPMENT OF CHICKS IN EGGS

Though Nature's way is often the best, hens are very variable creatures. Sometimes they are deficient in heat, and one will hatch well and the next one badly with eggs taken from the same breeding pen. One will chill every egg and bring no chicks, or will break one or more and endanger the rest, or leave the nest and refuse to continue hatching, and that at a critical period.

At times no broody hen is available. Anyone, therefore, who wishes to hatch large numbers of chickens must have incubators to remedy the hen's deficiencies. Even when one prefers natural incubation it is well to have an artificial incubator at hand in case of a hen forsaking her nest, or in which to place eggs a day or so before hatching, lest the hen should break the eggs or crush the newly-hatched chicks. If the hen does her work well, and is a gentle creature as she often is, it is better not to take her from the nest after the eggs begin to chip. She may be looked at once or twice in the day and the egg shells removed. I prefer the hen to remain on the nest until all the chicks are hatched and for some hours or a whole day afterwards. The chicks are better without any food for twenty-four hours, and are warmer with the mother on the nest than if removed to a coop. If she is restless, as she sometimes is, if the hatch is a prolonged one, either the chicks should be removed to the warm drying box of an incubator, or in a cosy basket lined with hay near the fire; or the chicks should be allowed to stay, and the eggs late in hatching be removed to an incubator or to another hen.

ARTIFICIAL INCUBATION
Unless the incubator house is built on purpose, which
should have double walls to secure an equable temperature,
and windows with shutters on each side to admit light
but to shut out the sun's direct rays, the best place is
a dry cellar, or a room with a northern aspect which
keeps a fairly even temperature.
The most convenient size is for 100 hen eggs. The
correct temperature of the egg "drawer" as shown by
the thermometer when placed as directed is about 104oF,
but may vary from 102oF to 105oF with safety. The
machines should stand quite firm and be perfectly level,
when tested by a spirit level.
Eggs should be tested on the seventh day, as directed
before, and again on the fifteenth day. On this latter testing,
any eggs which have not made satisfactory progress, and
are addled or the chicks dead, should be removed, as they
otherwise foul the air in the incubator and damage the
rest. The egg containing the live chick is by this time
quite opaque except at the broad end, where the air cell is
plainly seen. The bad eggs are less opaque and often look
cloudy and irregular in colour.
When the chicks are hatching the incubator should not
be opened more than two or three times during the day,
and then only for a moment to remove those which are
quite dry and strong to the drying box, in which they should
remain for twenty-four hours without food. If there is no
separate drying box the chicks should be left in the incubator.
THE SMALL INCUBATOR
There are two or three small incubators on the market
which will produce satisfactory results with a limited number

Marsh Incubator

Vision Incubator

Figure 5.6   Examples of Small Incubators

of eggs. The "visual" type is quite popular, possibly the best known being the "Curfew", the "Vision (Reliable)" incubator and the "Marsh". They have a perspex or plastic top through which the eggs can be observed.

The instructions issued with the particular incubator should be followed closely. Experience suggests the following hints should be followed:

1. Use fresh eggs not more than seven days old. Mark them with the date in pencil, but use a felt pen to show the date when eggs are put into the incubator.

2. Eggs should be a normal, oval shape with strong, even shells (porous shells are not usually hatchable).

3. Locate the incubator in a room which is well insulated and free from sunshine or draughts (fluctuations in room temperatures are better avoided).

4. Keep the water tray topped up so that the eggs have adequate moisture.

5. Turn the eggs at regular intervals – usually twice per day.

6. When chicks start to hatch try to avoid opening the incubator.

7. Check the thermometer at regular intervals so that the incubator keeps steady at around 102oF.

8. Load the machine with a reasonable number of eggs; e.g. at least twenty, or so few chicks will be hatched that rearing will be uneconomical.

Success with an incubator requires care, and application of the rules issued with the machine. Checking for fertility is advisable at seven and fourteen days. Any bad/addled eggs should be removed. With experience it

Bristol Incubator

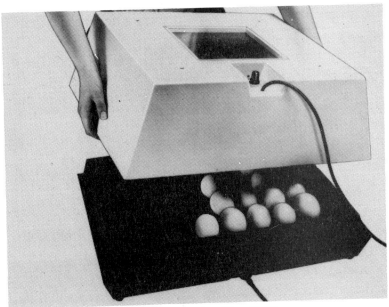

Brinsea Small Incubator

Figure 5.7 Other Small Incubators

becomes possible to use a strong torch and detect fertile eggs which have become "addled". However, in the early stages the beginner is advised to remove the "clears" only.

REARING CHICKS

Nature herself has provided food enough for the first few days in the yolk of the egg. This is not entirely used for building up the frame of the chick, but remains outside the abdomen, enclosed in a sac; the mouth of which is attached to the umbilical cord, and during the last few hours of the chick's life in the shell it is drawn into the abdomen to supply nourishment. I have known sickly chickens, that have refused to eat, live a whole week on this sustenance, and in a healthy growing chick traces of the yolk are to be found still for as long a period as ten days.

In the case of the hen, when she has finished hatching her brood, she should be well fed with maize or wheat, and be well dusted with insect powder to free her from lice. The dusting is best done, however, long before she finishes her task otherwise the chick be affected by the powder.

She should then be placed in a coop and the chickens be put to her. In cold weather eight or ten are quite enough for her to brood; in warm weather twelve or fifteen are not too many.

A hen which has been sitting for 28 days will take chickens from the incubator as readily as those she has hatched if they are placed with her own while she is on the nest, or if they are of the same colour as her own. A hen has no head for numbers, but a keen eye for colour, and if chicks of a different colour from her own are placed with them she will often kill them outright. She will also kill her neighbour's

79

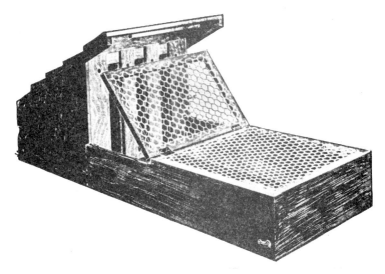

Small Coop (may be used to keep chicks in for 2–3 weeks)

Chicken House and Run

Figure 5.8   Typical Chicken Coops

80

A Modern Brooder (electricity) Bartholomews of Hampshire

Infra-Red Brooding

Figure 5.9 Brooders : Careful control of light and heat are vital requirements

81

chicks if they stray to her, unless they are of the same age and colour. I prefer to feed the young chicks on dry chick crumbs (or Turkey chick crumbs) entirely for the first ten or fourteen days. The morning meal may be of one of the well-known chick crumbs soaked in cold water, not warm or hot. There is a great tendency for any remnants of the latter to go sour and cause diarrhoea, which is the great scourge of chicken hood. For this reason any soft food left after the meal should be cleared away, and the coop in which the hen is kept should be moved to fresh ground daily. Give water ad lib., and always kept fresh and cool.

For artifically reared chicks the feeding is similar. There are many good brooders on the market, and the directions should be followed. I much prefer the brooders made with three divisions: (1) the warm compartment for sleeping, (2) the intermediate for feeding and exercise, and, (3) the outer run upon the grass, which is better covered, but with a wire-netted front. The best test that all is going well is when the chickens eat well and drink moderately, and when they lie about the sleeping compartment well spread about the whole of it and not huddled into one corner.

DANGERS

The chief dangers are: (1) overcrowding, (2) overheating, (3) draughts. All may be avoided by care. It is not well to place more than fifty in one rearer, and most of the brooders advertised to take fifty are much better with only thirty. As the chicks grow and take more space, great care should be taken against overcrowding.

In winter time they may remain in a brooder until six weeks old, but in warmer weather they may be removed to a cool brooder after a month.

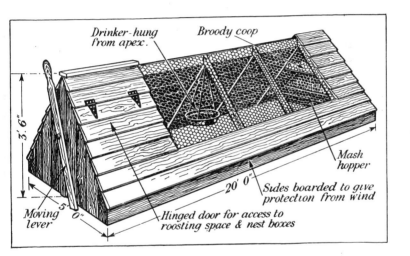

Figure 5.10   A Rearing Unit

Young Peafowl are quite hardy but are best kept within a pen until fully feathered. They become tame and disease and predators are avoided.

Infra-Red Lamp

Brooders may be heated by oil lamp, electric element or infra-red lamp. The latter is very effective and cheap to operate. However, access to natural light is recommended or the chicks will suffer from eye problems. An outside run will allow the chicks to leave the area of the lamp.

A home-made appliance may have a wooden or earth floor and water proof top, with fine wire-netting on the sides. The lamp is suspended from the top and raised or lowered to vary the temperature reaching the chicks.

If the chicks huddle together they are too cold, whereas, if "mopy" they are probably overheated and lack vitality.

How to grow the chicks

The secret of successful rearing is to keep the chicks growing from first to last without any check. To do this, care must be exercised to keep them from colds and other chicken ailments, free from insect pests, and to give them suitable food and comfortable housing. Until they are a month old they should be fed five or six times a day; after that, until three months old, four times; and from then until maturity, three times. The heat should be around 95oF and this should be reduced 5 degrees F. each week. At six to eight weeks they may be moved to an indoor brooder without heat.

Sometimes a table is used to indicate temperature required and can be useful for watching the chicks.

NOTE

The tabulation opposite may be used as a guide, but much depends on the time of year and prevailing weather.

Degrees F	Age
90	day old
90–85	lst week
85–80	2nd week
80–75	3rd week
75–65	4th week
65	5th week

For the evening meal whole wheat, oats or kibbled – (i.e. cracked) maize, alternately.

For those who do not want the trouble of mixing foods ready–made growers' pellets, crumbs or mash may be obtained from a specialist supplier.

A good ration for birds from three months onwards is:

1. Scalded biscuit meal, 1 part   or
   Pea meal, 1 part
   Sharps, 2 parts

2. Ground oats, 1 part
   Sharps, 2 parts
   Maize meal, 1 part

AILMENTS

Chicks are surprisingly strong. However, they cannot thrive under conditions which are cold and damp. Given appropriate accommodation they will grow quickly.

The main dangers are predators such as rats, and chick ailments, especially coccidiosis. A careful watch should be maintained for any sign of rats. All possible access points should be covered.

TREATMENT OF EGGS

Disease can be transmitted from the eggs to the chicks. In addition, eggs can be contaminated from being soiled and may turn putrid before hatching. One of the main problems is Yolk–sac infection.

The infected yolk is absorbed by the chick and fails to

maintain it adequately so that it probably dies within a week of hatching.

If this is to be avoided, strict rules of hygiene must be observed. Alternative procedures are possible:

1. Wash each egg with water to which has been added an effective but mild disinfectant.
2. Dip each egg in a special sterilising solution. (May have to be combined with (1) above).
3. Fumigate eggs using formalin, but care must be taken not to kill the embryo germ (not recommended).
4. Nest boxes should be cleaned regularly and fresh sawdust and straw added.
5. Eggs should be stored correctly in clean conditions at a temperature of 55 to 60oF and turned each day.

For more detailed diseases and procedures readers are referred to: " Poultry Diseases Under Modern Management" ,G.S. Coutts, Nimrod Press.

6

MORE DETAILED
DESCRIPTIONS

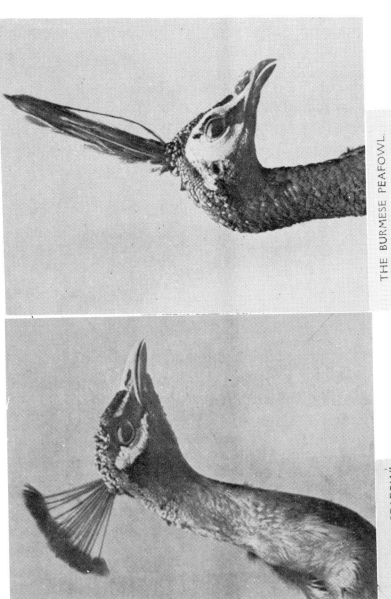

THE BURMESE PEAFOWL.

THE INDIAN PEAFOWL.

Figure 6.1 Photographs to illustrate the tail and train
Note: the tail proper is long and wedge shaped with twenty feathers. The train is extremely

MORE DETAILED DESCRIPTIONS*

OUTLINE DESCRIPTIONS

For a brief description of the main species the reader is referred to Chapter 1. In this chapter the descriptions of the main species are now enlarged using the works of various authorities (see Bibliography).

COMMON BLUE PEAFOWL (Pavo cristatus)

ADULT MALE

Feathered portion of the head dark metallic green–blue, gradually changing to brilliant Prussian blue on neck, breast and shoulders, shaded in different lights with green and purple–blue; lower breast deeper purple–blue, changing to deep metallic green on abdomen and flanks and, again, to dull brownish–black on vent, centre of abdomen and under tail–coverts; back from shoulders to rump brilliant light bronze–green, each feather black–edged, those nearest the neck with blue central streaks, and those of the rump with wide sub–edges of metallic golden–green; tail dark brown with paler mottling near the shafts; central upper tail–coverts, composing the train, bronze–green with a copper sheen near the tips, each feather with an eye formed by a deep blue

* Readers are referred to The Peafowl of the World by Josef Bergmann. Where coloured illustrations are given and comparisons are made.

heart–shaped spot with four rings; the first ring a narrow one of brilliant smalt blue–green; the second, much broader, of golden bronze, then a very narrow one of gold, and finally one of brown. The outer feathers and the longest of the central ones have no eyes, but terminate in a broad half-moon. A few of the outer shorter coverts have indefinite ocelli of deep copper colour.

Wings: Primaries, their greater coverts and bastard wing, pale chestnut–brown; outer secondaries, with their greater and median coverts, dark brown glossed with deep metallic blue, most pronounced on the median coverts; inner secondaries, all other coverts and scapulars buff with dark brown bars, definite and glossed with green on the scapulars and coverts next them, broken and with practically no gloss elsewhere.

Colours of the Soft Parts: Bare portion of the face and cheeks livid white; bill dark horny, darkest at the tip and along culmen; lower mandible paler; iris dark hazel–brown; legs and feet greyish brown to dark horny–brown; claws still darker.

ADULT FEMALE

Top of the head mostly dark chestnut, each feather bordered with golden–brown, becoming paler on the neck; mantle golden–green; remainder of the uppper plumage brownish marked and barred with brownish white or buff; primary quills and tail-feathers dark brown with paler tips, lower breast and abdomen whitish buff.

YOUNG MALES

Young males resemble the adult female but have th

primary quills pale chestnut, as in the males, though mottled with dark brown.

YOUNG BIRD, NINE WEEKS OLD

Top of head pale sandy with black bases to the feathers, crest about 1/2 inch long, black at the base, brownish chestnut on the terminal half and tipped with black; general colour of the upper parts, including the wings and tail, light brown, barred and freckled with brownish black; under-surface of the body yellowish white becoming browner on the chest.

CHICK IN DOWN

Pale buff with dark brown nuchal mark running from behind one eye to the other and down across the neck; back deeper rufous brown; quills of wing pale dull chestnut mottled with brown, secondaries barred and mottled with brown and pale tipped.

BLACK WINGED

The form known as *nigripenris* differs from the common one having the scapulars and wing-coverts black with narrow green edges; the thighs are black and the back is still more golden than in the normal plumage

There is nothing to prove that this form is other than an abnormal phase, showing, perhaps, an inclination towards-melanism. It is very rare and has hitherto never been obtained in birds in a state of nature. Grant suggests that the coloration may be a reversion to the original ancestor of all

Peafowl, but there is no proof of its being an atavism, and it appears to me that some tendency to melanism is a more likely cause.

WHITE

Albinoism is very common, even in a wild state, many such birds having been shot, whilst in a domestic state the form has become a permanent one, breeding true with great regularity.

GREEN PEAFOWL *(Pavo muticus)*

Originally naturists referred to this bird as the **Burmese Peafowl**, but nowadays recognition is given to the Java Peafowl (*Pavo muticus muticus*) and Indo-China Peafowl (*Pavo muticus imperiton*).
The description which follows may be applied to them all.

ADULT MALE

Head from forehead to nape, lores, chin and throat brilliant metallic blue-green, with a purple sheen in some lights; neck and extreme upper breast and mantle golden-bronze, the centre of each feather deep purple -blue, bordered with verdigris-green and obsoletely fringed with the same. On the **neck** the blue centres are hidden, but on the **upper mantle** they show prominently and, on this part, the feathers are boldly fringed with black. **Back**: brilliant emerald-green, each feather edged with black, and centred with bronze. **Below**, the breast is bronze, each feather edged with deep blue-green and centred with the same; remainder of lower parts and flanks duller, deeper green fading to dull brownish-black on the centre of the abdomen, vent and under tail-coverts.

under tail-coverts.

Wing-coverts next the scapulars bronze-green with deep blue centres and dark margins; other coverts deep metallic blue-green, changing to copper bronze on the coverts of the inner secondaries; bastard wing, greater coverts and primaries light chestnut, with dark brown shafts and tips; secondaries dark brown with metallic green lustre on the visible portions; tail dark brown with paler mottlings next to the shaft; tail-coverts which form the train similar to those of the Common Peacock.

Colours of Soft Parts – Naked skin round the eye bluish green, cheeks yellow to pale orange; bill dark horny-brown, darkest at the tip and paler at base of lower mandible; legs and feet dark grey-brown or horny-brown, claws blackish; iris dark brown or deep hazel-brown.

ADULT FEMALE

Has no train and differs from the male in the following respects: The whole back and rump are brownish black, more or less barred and marked with buff, the feathers next the scapulars with faint metallic green edges. The feathers of the breast have the bronze and black borders more broken up in appearance. The primaries, bastard wing and greater coverts are more less mottled on the outer webs. The upper tail-coverts are no longer than the tail and are much mixed with brown and light buff. Tail brown with narrow bars and tips of paler brown.

YOUNG MALE

Resembles the adult female, but the feathers of the lower back are greenish bronze and the upper tail-coverts are golden-green tipped with bronze. They fall short of the tip of the tail by about 6 inches.

The young male soon commences to show the sexual differences in coloration, though the metallic parts are more bronze and less green than in the adult. The primaries and their coverts remain like those of the female, whilst the secondaries and the coverts are dark brown with narrow pale bars, the inner webs much mottled with buff. The green part shows as a metallic sheen on the darker markings. The longer upper tail-coverts are mostly a brilliant copper flame-colour broken by the narrow buff bars and by faint indications of the green gloss.

The crest, even when of practically full size, is dull-coloured and nearly entirely blackish brown.

In the Burmese Peafowl the reflections on the metallic parts vary greatly in different lights , in some the green predominates, whilst in others the deep blue almost alone shows, whilst in certain lights the whole tail looks almost copper-coloured.

BURMESE PEAFOWL
ADDITIONAL NOTES (Hume and Marshall)

I have not many measurements of this species, but I note that birds, even in full plumage, seem to vary much in size according to age.

The total length of the finest bird of which I have a record, from the tip of the bill to the end of the train, was 90 inches. The following are the details of all the males we have measured and weighed in the flesh:-

Length, to end of true tail, 40.0 to 48.0; train, projects beyond end of tail from 24.0 to 44.0 ; expanse, 50.5 to 60.0; wing, 16.75 to 19,75; tail from vent, 15.5 to 17.5; tarsus, 5.5 to 6.3; bill from gape, 1.95 to 2.5. Weight, 8.5 to 11.0 lbs.

Legs and feet dark horny brown; bill dark horny brown; lower mandible pale near base, irides dark brown.

The facial skin is of two colours – smalt blue and chrome yellow.

The blue runs from a point in front of and below the nostrils, where it is palest, to the gape, and from thence in a curved line past, and 0.125 in front, of the orifice of the ear to within 0.35 of the top of the head, from thence curving round over the eye, and about 0.2 above it, down to the point below the nostrils already referred to; the blue is brightest just behind the eye.

The chrome yellow extends as a broad irregular band over the posterior portion of the face, immediately behind the blue. It is widest on the cheeks, where it may be 0.8 wide, and narrowest at the aural orifice, which it encloses, where it may be 0.45 wide. It begins at the gape and goes up as high as the blue. A broad patch of small scaly metallic green feathers runs across the blue from near the gape up to and just touching the lower margin of the eye. A line of similar feathers runs immediately over the eye, curving up a little posteriorly.

A tiny patch of somewhat similar feathers above the aural orifice, and it is about this part that the chrome yellow is brightest; at the line of junction of the blue and yellow, the colours become slightly inter-mingled, the blue being perceptibly tinged with yellow, and the yellow with blue, producing a dirty greenish shade.

P CRISTATUS

Lastly, whereas in *P. cristatus* all the lesser wing-coverts, the tertiaries and all their coverts, and the scapulars, are conspicuously barred and variegated with black on a rufescent or buffy white ground; in *muticus* these parts are uniform and unbarred.

ORNITHOLOGIST'S FOOTNOTE

Charles Inglis observed these birds in the wild and in his copy of Hume and Marshall has annotated that:

**The facial colours are intensified in the breeding season. Moreover, the "blue has a purplish tinge". Both the blue and yellow are brighter with the yellow being "orangey".
The plumage is also brighter at this period.**

The reader is referred to the illustrations which show the difference between the two main species.

AVICULTURIST'S NOTE

Breeders like Delacour have made a study of breeding Peafowl and the colours which may be obtained. They have noted the likely effects of producing hybrids on the colours available. If we view the manner in which the colours of poultry and aviary birds have multiplied it is surprising that so few colours exist. Notes gathered are:

1. Whites occur in the wild as well as in domestication. However their chicks tend to be delicate and should be given extra care.

2. The Indian Peafowl crossed with its "sport", the White, will produce Blues with a few white flights. Crossed with together should produce 25 per cent white, 25 per cent blue and 50 per cent a mixture. This is the normal Mendel's expectation .

3. A Pied (mixture of colour) is also bred which tends to become variegated. When crossed with white quite attractive birds are produced. However, crossing with Blue results in

Blues with White splashes which are not really attractive.

4. The Green Peafowl (Pavo   muticus) is not as hardy as the Blue Peafowl and ,therefore, should be watched very carefully when weather is quite severe ; eg heavy snows and frost.

SOURCE OF DETAILS

The Game-Birds of India, Burma and Ceylon,
E. C. Stuart Baker, Bombay Natural History Society, 1930

The Game - Birds of India, Burmah and Ceylon,
Hume and Marshall, Privately Published, 1879

The Pheasants of the World , J. Delacour.
Nimrod Press, 1989

Aviculture Magazine for various years
(The Avicultural Society)

APPENDIX

Sources of Supplies and Index

KEEPING PEAFOWL

Various companies and firms supply food and equipment for cage birds and some of these are as follows (they are also quoted in the text with appropriate equipment):

Bartholomews of Hampshire
Fyning, Rogate, West Sussex.
Tubular heaters, hospital cages, etc.

Haines Aviary Economy
28 Horsewell Lane, Wigston Magna, Leicester
Hoppers, Winnowing Machines, nest boxes, etc.

Shaws Pet Products Ltd
50 West Road, Aston Clinton, Aylesbury, Bucks
A wide range of supplements

Sinderins Electronic Products
Sheiron House, Memus, Forfar, DD8 3UA
Dimmers for controlled lighting

Prestige Technology Ltd
Thetford, Norfolk
Negative Air Ionisers for Birdrooms

Porters Pet Stores
81 Platchett Grove, London, E6
Cage fronts, show cages, foods and appliances

Ponderosa Bird Aviaries
The Reddings, Cheltenham, Glos.
Cages, food and various appliances

THE PARROT SOCIETY

Those interested in parrot-like birds are advised to join The Parrot Society, 108b Fenlake Road, Bedford, MK42 0EU, England